MARKS &
SPENCER

mediterranean

simple and delicious easy-to-make recipes

Lorraine Turner

Marks and Spencer p.l.c.
Baker Street, London, W1U 8EP

www.marksandspencer.com

Copyright © Exclusive Editions 2002

ISBN: 1-84273-812-7

Printed in China

Produced by the Bridgewater Book Company Ltd.

Photographer Calvey Taylor-Haw

Home Economist Sharon Riddick

NOTES FOR THE READER

- This book uses both metric and imperial measurements. Follow the same units of measurement throughout; do not mix metric and imperial.

- All spoon measurements are level: teaspoons are assumed to be 5 ml, and tablespoons are assumed to be 15 ml.

- Unless otherwise stated, milk is assumed to be full fat, eggs and individual vegetables such as potatoes are medium, and pepper is freshly ground black pepper.

- Recipes using raw or very lightly cooked eggs should be avoided by infants, the elderly, pregnant women, convalescents, and anyone suffering from an illness.

- The times given are an approximate guide only. Preparation times differ according to the techniques used by different people and the cooking times may also vary from those given.

contents

introduction

Mediterranean cooking is more popular than ever and offers a spectacular array of possibilities. Its dishes span many different countries and cultures, from France and the sun-drenched coasts of Spain and Italy, to eastern European and North African countries such as Turkey and Morocco.

This book presents a stunning selection of recipes from the region, beginning with delicious soups and starters, and progressing to an exciting selection of fish, poultry and meat main courses. There is also a section full of mouthwatering vegetarian dishes and salads, and a chapter that features some irresistible desserts.

All the recipes in this book are presented with full-colour photographs and are clearly explained in step-by-step detail. They use readily available ingredients and are packed with aromas and spices that will soon bring the ambience of this beautiful part of the world into your kitchen, so that you will be able to enjoy authentic Mediterranean flavours wherever you happen to be. With the ever-increasing availability of delicious fruits and vegetables, oils and vinegars, and herbs and spices at our fingertips, there has never been a better time to explore Mediterranean cooking.

guide to recipe key		
	very easy	Recipes are graded as follows: 1 pea = easy; 2 peas = very easy; 3 peas = extremely easy.
	serves 4	Recipes generally serve four people. Simply halve the ingredients to serve two, taking care not to mix metric and imperial measurements.
	10 minutes	Preparation time. Where marinating or soaking are involved, these times have been added on separately: eg, 15 minutes + 30 minutes to marinate.
	10 minutes	Cooking time. Cooking times don't include the cooking of side dishes or accompaniments served with the main dishes.

serrano ham & mushroom salad
page 24

lamb kebabs
page 54

italian salad
page 80

chocolate gelato
page 86

soups
& starters

The warm, sunny Mediterranean climate produces wonderful fruits, vegetables and herbs, and what better way to begin this section than with a deliciously refreshing chilled Gazpacho from Spain, with juicy sun-ripened tomatoes, fragrant olive oil and the wonderful flavour of fresh garlic? This chapter is full of tempting ingredients from this part of the world, which are guaranteed to tantalise every palate.

gazpacho

extremely easy	**ingredients**	
serves 4	500 g/1 lb 2 oz large ripe tomatoes 4 tbsp extra-virgin olive oil 1 onion, chopped 1 red pepper, deseeded and chopped 1 orange pepper, deseeded and chopped	3 garlic cloves, chopped 1 cucumber, peeled and chopped salt and pepper sprigs of fresh basil, to garnish
15 minutes + 3–4 hours to chill		
—		

First skin the tomatoes. Bring a kettle of water to the boil. Put the tomatoes into a heatproof bowl, then pour over enough boiling water to cover them. Let them soak for 2–4 minutes, then lift them out of the water and allow to cool slightly.

When the tomatoes are cool enough to handle, gently pierce the skins with the point of a knife. You should now find the skins easy to remove. Discard the skins, halve the tomatoes and remove the seeds. Chop the tomatoes and place them in a food processor.

Add the oil, onion, red and orange peppers and garlic to the food processor. Add all but 2 tablespoons of the chopped cucumber, and reserve the rest in the refrigerator. Season with salt and pepper and process until smooth. Strain through a sieve into a large bowl, cover with clingfilm and refrigerate for 3–4 hours.

Serve chilled, garnished with the remaining chopped cucumber and sprigs of fresh basil.

provençal soup
with pistou sauce

		ingredients	
	very easy	2 tbsp extra-virgin olive oil	75 g/2¾ oz dried small soup pasta
		1 garlic clove, chopped	1 tsp dried mixed herbs
	serves 4	1 onion, chopped	salt and pepper
		450 g/1 lb potatoes	
		1 large carrot, chopped	PISTOU SAUCE
		1.2 litres/2 pints vegetable stock	60 g/2¼ oz fresh basil
	20 minutes	100 g/3½ oz thin French beans	3 tbsp freshly grated Parmesan
		100 g/3½ oz canned red kidney beans	4 tbsp extra-virgin olive oil
		2 tomatoes, skinned (see page 8)	2 garlic cloves, chopped
	20 minutes	100 g/3½ oz frozen peas	shavings of fresh Parmesan, to garnish
		100 g/3½ oz cooked ham, chopped	

To make the pistou sauce, reserve 4 sprigs of basil for garnish and blend the rest in a food processor with the Parmesan, olive oil and garlic. Transfer to a bowl, cover with clingfilm and chill until required.

For the soup, heat the oil in a large pan over a low heat. Add the garlic and onion and cook for 4 minutes, stirring, until softened slightly. Chop the potatoes and add them with the carrot, then stir in the stock. Bring to the boil, then reduce the heat and simmer for about 10 minutes, or until the vegetables are starting to soften.

Top and tail the French beans, cut them into small pieces, and drain the kidney beans. Chop the tomatoes. Add the French beans, kidney beans and tomatoes to the pan with the peas, ham, pasta and mixed herbs. Season well and cook for a further 5 minutes, or until the vegetables and pasta are tender.

Remove from the heat. Stir in the pistou sauce. Transfer to serving bowls. Garnish with Parmesan and the reserved sprigs of basil.

avgolemono

easy	**ingredients**	
serves 4	1.4 litres/2½ pints water 650 g/1 lb 7 oz chicken meat 1 celery stick, trimmed and sliced 1 onion, sliced 2 garlic cloves, peeled 1 bouquet garni 100 g/3½ oz rice	2 egg yolks 3 tbsp lemon juice salt and pepper GARNISH slices of lemon, quartered sprigs of fresh flat-leaved parsley
15 minutes		
2½ hours		

Put the water, chicken, celery, onion, garlic and bouquet garni into a large pan and bring to the boil. Reduce the heat and skim away surface scum. Partially cover, and simmer for 2 hours. Allow to cool.

Lift out the chicken, bouquet garni and large vegetable pieces. Chop 300 g/10½ oz of the chicken meat, cover with clingfilm and set aside. Discard the rest, and the other solids. Skim away any remaining fat from the stock. Strain the stock into a bowl through a sieve lined with clean muslin. Transfer all but 10 fl oz to a pan and bring to the boil. Add the rice and cook over a medium heat for 25 minutes. Add the reserved chopped chicken.

In a separate bowl, whisk together the egg yolks and lemon juice. Gradually whisk in 6 tablespoons of reserved stock, then another 200 ml/7 fl oz. Slowly pour the mixture back into the pan, stirring. Remove from the heat before it starts to boil and season to taste. Ladle into serving bowls and garnish with lemon slices and sprigs of parsley.

taramasalata

		ingredients	
easy	150 g/5½ oz skinless cod's roe 2 garlic cloves, finely chopped 2 shallots, finely chopped	GARNISH slices of lemon, quartered sprig of fresh flat-leaved parsley	
serves 4	6 tbsp lemon juice 1 tbsp finely grated lemon rind 4 slices of fresh white bread, crusts removed	TO SERVE warm pitta breads shredded fresh green salad leaves slices of fresh tomato	
15 minutes	salt and pepper 125 ml/4 fl oz olive oil		
—			

Put the cod's roe, garlic, shallots, and lemon juice and rind into a food processor and blend together well. Break the bread into small pieces and add it to the mixture. Season with salt and pepper and blend until smooth.

With the motor running, gradually pour the olive oil through the feed tube and blend until smooth. Transfer the mixture to a bowl, cover with clingfilm and chill until required.

When ready to serve, garnish the taramasalata with lemon slices and a sprig of fresh flat-leaved parsley, and serve with pitta breads, green salad leaves and fresh tomato slices.

hummus

		ingredients	

	very easy	400 g/14 oz dried chickpeas
		4 garlic cloves, chopped
		200 ml/7 fl oz sesame oil
		5 tbsp tahini
		3 tbsp lemon juice
		pinch of cayenne
		salt and pepper
			sprigs of fresh flat-leaved parsley,
			   to garnish
			
			TO SERVE
			pitta breads, halved and opened to
			   make 'pockets'
			fresh green salad leaves
			slices of cucumber
			slices of fresh tomato

	serves 4		
	10 minutes + 8 hours to soak		
	1½ hours		

Put the chickpeas in a large bowl and add enough cold water to cover them when they have doubled in size. Cover with clingfilm and soak for at least 8 hours or overnight.

Drain the chickpeas and transfer to a large pan. Cover well with water, and bring to the boil. Boil vigorously for at least 10 minutes, then reduce the heat and simmer for 1¼ hours until tender. Skim away any surface scum if necessary. Drain and leave to cool.

Put the garlic, sesame oil, tahini, lemon juice and cayenne in a food processor and blend until smooth. Add the chickpeas and process to a thick purée, adding a little water to thin the mixture if necessary. Season with salt and pepper.

Transfer to a serving bowl, cover with clingfilm and chill until required. When ready to use, garnish with sprigs of fresh flat-leaved parsley and serve with pitta breads stuffed with fresh salad leaves and cucumber and tomato slices.

tzatziki

extremely easy	
serves 4	
10 minutes + 2 hours to chill	
—	

ingredients

500 ml/18 fl oz natural Greek-style
   yogurt, or other thick natural yogurt
4 garlic cloves, very finely chopped
2 medium cucumbers, peeled,
   deseeded and very finely diced
1 tbsp lemon-flavoured or extra-virgin
   olive oil
3 tbsp lemon juice
1 tbsp chopped fresh mint leaves
salt and pepper

pinch of paprika, to garnish

TO SERVE
celery stalks, cut into sticks
carrots, cut into sticks
pitta bread, cut into triangles

Put the yogurt, garlic, cucumber, oil, lemon juice and mint into a serving bowl and stir together until well combined. Season with salt and pepper, cover with clingfilm, and chill for at least 2 hours, or until required.

When ready to use, garnish with a pinch of paprika. Serve with celery, carrots and pitta bread triangles for dipping.

bagna cauda

very easy	
serves 4	
5 minutes	
20 minutes	

ingredients

6 tbsp olive oil
6 tbsp butter
4 garlic cloves, chopped
100 g/3 ½ oz canned anchovy fillets in
oil, drained and chopped
6 tbsp single cream

TO SERVE
blanched asparagus spears
blanched broccoli florets
strips of red pepper
strips of pitta bread

Heat the oil in a fondue pot over a low heat, add the butter and stir until melted. Add the garlic and cook, stirring continuously, for 4 minutes.

Add the anchovies and cook, stirring, for about 12–15 minutes, then stir in the cream. Keep the dip warm in the fondue pot over a very low heat while you pass round a selection of asparagus, broccoli, red pepper and pitta bread strips for dipping.

pissaladière

		ingredients	
easy	4 tbsp olive oil	PASTRY
	4 garlic cloves, chopped	150 g/5½ oz plain flour, plus extra
serves 4	900 g/2 lb onions, sliced	for dusting
	pinch of ground cloves	pinch of salt
	2 tomatoes, sliced into wedges	5 tbsp butter, chopped
15 minutes	50 g/1¾ oz canned anchovy fillets in	2 tbsp cold water
+ 1½ hours	oil, drained and cut into strips	
to chill	50 g/1¾ oz black olives, stoned	GARNISH
	and quartered	1 tbsp chopped fresh thyme
	50 g/1¾ oz green olives, stoned	black olives, stoned and halved
45 minutes	and quartered	crisp green salad leaves, to serve

To make the pastry, rub the flour and salt together in a large bowl. Rub in the butter to form fine crumbs. Mix in the cold water. Knead lightly, wrap in clingfilm and chill for at least 1½ hours.

Preheat the oven to 200°C/400°F/Gas Mark 6. Roll out the dough to a thickness of 5 mm/¼ inch. Use it to line a 20-cm/8-inch flan tin. Prick all over with a fork, line with baking paper and fill with baking beans. Bake in the preheated oven for 15 minutes.

Meanwhile, heat the oil in a large frying pan over a very low heat. Add the garlic, onions and cloves and cook, stirring, for 15 minutes.

Remove the pastry from the oven; discard the paper and baking beans. Arrange the onion mixture and tomatoes over the pastry. Top with the anchovies and olive quarters. Bake for 30 minutes.

Remove from the oven and garnish with chopped fresh thyme and black olive halves. Serve with a crisp green salad.

serrano ham & mushroom salad

		ingredients	
	extremely easy	½ small galia melon, peeled and sliced	3 tbsp lemon juice
		12 very thin slices of Serrano ham, cut into strips	4 tbsp olive oil
	serves 4	6 ripe fresh figs, trimmed and quartered	pepper
	15 minutes	150 g/5½ oz white mushrooms	sprigs of fresh flat-leaved parsley, to garnish
		1 avocado	
	—		

Divide the melon slices, ham strips and fig quarters between serving plates. Wipe the mushrooms clean with a damp, clean cloth, then slice them thickly and scatter them over the top.

Using a knife, cut the avocado in half and remove the stone. Remove and discard the skin, and cut the flesh into slices. Brush the slices with 1 tablespoon of the lemon juice to prevent discoloration, then arrange them over the top of the salad.

In a separate bowl, pour in the remaining lemon juice and all the olive oil and stir until thoroughly mixed. Season with pepper. Pour the mixture over the salad, ensuring that all the salad ingredients are well coated. Garnish with sprigs of fresh parsley and serve.

olive & sun-dried tomato bread

<table>
<tr><td></td><td colspan="2">ingredients</td></tr>
<tr>
<td>easy</td>
<td>400 g/14 oz plain flour, plus extra
  for dusting
1 tsp salt</td>
<td>4 tbsp olive oil, plus extra for greasing
50 g/1¾ oz black olives, stoned and
  sliced</td>
</tr>
<tr>
<td>serves 4</td>
<td>1 sachet easy-blend dried yeast
1 tsp brown sugar
1 tbsp chopped fresh thyme</td>
<td>50 g/1¾ oz green olives, stoned and
  sliced
100 g/3½ oz sun-dried tomatoes in oil,</td>
</tr>
<tr>
<td>20 minutes
+ 2¼ hours
to rise</td>
<td>200 ml/7 fl oz warm water (heated
  to 50°C/122°F)</td>
<td> drained and sliced
1 egg yolk, beaten</td>
</tr>
<tr>
<td>40 minutes</td>
<td></td>
<td></td>
</tr>
</table>

Stir together the flour, salt and yeast in a bowl, then stir in the sugar and thyme. Make a well in the centre. Slowly stir in enough water and oil to make a dough. Mix in the olives and sun-dried tomatoes. Knead the dough for 5 minutes, then form it into a ball. Brush a bowl with oil, add the dough and cover with clingfilm. Leave to rise in a warm place for about 1½ hours until doubled in size.

Dust a baking sheet with flour. Knead the dough lightly, then cut into two halves and shape into ovals or rounds. Put them on the baking sheet, cover with clingfilm and leave to rise again in a warm place for about 45 minutes until doubled in size.

Preheat the oven to 200°C/400°F/Gas Mark 6. Make 3 shallow diagonal cuts on the top of each piece of dough. Brush with the egg. Bake for 40 minutes or until cooked through – they should be golden on top and sound hollow when tapped on the bottom. Transfer to wire racks to cool. Store in an airtight container for up to 3 days.

fish, poultry & meat

The Mediterranean area is famed for its fish and shellfish, and it also produces some wonderful poultry and meat dishes. Who could resist juicy Mediterranean mussels oozing with olive oil, lemon, garlic and white wine? Or lamb kebabs cooked with melting Gruyère cheese and fragrant rosemary? This section offers some truly spectacular and satisfying dishes to inspire every cook and enhance any dinner menu.

seafood salad

	ingredients	
very easy	250 g/9 oz live mussels	1 tbsp lemon juice
	350 g/12 oz scallops	1 garlic clove, finely chopped
serves 4	250 g/9 oz cleaned squid, cut into rings and tentacles	1 tbsp chopped fresh parsley
		salt and pepper
	1 red onion, halved and finely sliced	
15 minutes + 45 minutes to chill	300 g/10½ oz fresh asparagus, blanched and cut into small pieces	GARNISH
		sprigs of fresh flat-leaved parsley
		wedges of lemon
	DRESSING	capers (optional)
8–10 minutes	4 tbsp extra-virgin olive oil	whole cooked baby squid (optional)
	2 tbsp white wine vinegar	

Soak the mussels in salted water for 10 minutes. Scrub under cold running water and pull off any beards. Discard any with broken shells. Tap the remaining mussels: discard any that refuse to close. Put the closed mussels into a large pan with a little water, bring to the boil and cook over a high heat for 4 minutes. Drain into a large bowl and reserve the liquid. Discard any mussels that remain closed, refresh the rest of the mussels under cold water, drain and set aside.

Return the reserved liquid to the pan and bring to the boil. Add the scallops and squid and cook for 3 minutes. Remove from the heat, drain, refresh under cold running water and drain again. Remove the mussels from their shells. Put them in a bowl with the scallops and squid, allow to cool, cover with clingfilm and chill for 45 minutes.

Arrange the seafood on serving plates. Top with onion and asparagus. Mix the dressing ingredients and drizzle over the salad. Garnish with parsley and lemon wedges, and capers and whole baby squid if using.

salade niçoise

		ingredients	
very easy			
	4 eggs		DRESSING
	200 g/7 oz French beans		5 tbsp extra-virgin olive oil
serves 4	1 green pepper, deseeded and sliced		3 tbsp red wine vinegar
	4 tomatoes, cut into wedges		½ tsp honey
	1 red onion, halved and sliced		1 garlic clove, chopped
20 minutes	1 tbsp chopped fresh parsley		salt and pepper
+ 20 minutes	1 tbsp chopped fresh coriander		
to cool	50 g/1¾ oz black olives, stoned		GARNISH
	400 g/14 oz canned tuna in brine		capers
10–12	50 g/1¾ oz anchovy fillets in oil		sprigs of fresh parsley
minutes			

Bring two pans of water to the boil. Add the eggs to one pan, bring back to the boil, reduce the heat and cook for 10 minutes. While the eggs are cooking, trim the French beans and put them in the other pan. Bring to the boil and blanch for 3 minutes, then drain and plunge into cold water. Drain again and leave to cool. When the eggs are cooked, drain and plunge them into cold water. Drain again and leave to cool.

To make the dressing, combine all the ingredients in a small bowl. Season and stir together well.

Divide the pepper, tomatoes, onion, parsley and coriander between serving dishes. Halve the olives and the French beans, shell and quarter the eggs, and add them all to the salad. Drain the tuna and anchovies and add to the salad. Drizzle over the dressing and garnish with capers and sprigs of fresh parsley. Cover with clingfilm and chill in the refrigerator until required.

galician cod

		ingredients	
very easy	900 g/2 lb potatoes, sliced		1 tsp cayenne
	150 g/5½ oz fine green beans		1 tbsp chopped fresh flat-leaved
	4 cod fillets, about 175 g/6 oz each		parsley
serves 4			salt and pepper
	DRESSING		
	6 tbsp olive oil		GARNISH
10 minutes	1 onion, chopped		capers
	2 garlic cloves, chopped		sprigs of fresh flat-leaved parsley
	1 tbsp sherry vinegar		
15–20 minutes			

Bring a saucepan of lightly salted water to the boil. Add the potatoes, bring back to the boil, reduce the heat to medium and cook for about 15 minutes or until tender.

Meanwhile, bring two pans of lightly salted water to the boil. Put the green beans in one pan and the fish in the other. Bring back to the boil, reduce the heat to low and simmer for 5 minutes.

While the fish and vegetables are cooking, make the dressing. Heat the oil in a saucepan over a medium heat. Add the onion and garlic and cook, stirring, for 3 minutes or until softened. Remove from the heat and pour in the sherry vinegar, then stir in the cayenne and parsley. Season with salt and pepper.

Drain the potatoes, green beans and fish separately. Arrange the potatoes on individual serving plates, cover them with beans and top with a cod fillet. Spoon over the warm dressing, garnish with capers and sprigs of parsley, and serve.

paella

		ingredients	
easy	3 tbsp olive oil	4 skinless, boneless chicken breasts
	2 tbsp butter	150 g/5½ oz lean chorizo, skinned
serves 4	2 garlic cloves, chopped	200 g/7 oz cooked lobster meat
	1 onion, chopped	200 g/7 oz prawns, peeled and
	2 large tomatoes, deseeded and diced	deveined
	150 g/5½ oz arborio rice	1 tbsp chopped flat-leaved parsley
15 minutes	85 g/3 oz frozen peas	salt and pepper
	1 red pepper, deseeded and chopped	
	2 tsp dried mixed herbs	GARNISH
30 minutes	1 tsp powdered saffron	pinch of cayenne
	425 ml/15 fl oz chicken stock	strips of red pepper

Heat the oil and butter in a large frying pan over a medium heat. Add the garlic and onion and cook, stirring, for about 3 minutes, until slightly softened.

Add the tomatoes, rice, peas, red pepper, mixed herbs and saffron and cook, stirring, for 2 minutes. Pour in the stock and bring to the boil. Reduce the heat to low and cook, stirring, for 10 minutes.

Chop the chicken and add to the pan. Cook, stirring occasionally, for 5 minutes. Chop the chorizo, add to the pan and cook for 3 minutes. Chop the lobster meat and add to the pan with the prawns and parsley. Season with salt and pepper and cook, stirring, for a further 2 minutes.

Remove from the heat, transfer to a large serving platter or individual serving plates, garnish with cayenne and strips of red pepper, and serve.

cioppino

		ingredients	
easy		3 tbsp olive oil	350 g/12 oz cod fillets
		2 tbsp butter	350 g/12 oz prawns, peeled and
serves 4		2 garlic cloves, chopped	deveined
		1 onion, chopped	200 g/7 oz cooked lobster meat, cut
		400 g/14 oz canned chopped tomatoes	into chunks
15 minutes		450 ml/16 fl oz fish stock	salt and pepper
		200 ml/7 fl oz dry white wine	sprigs of fresh flat-leaved parsley,
		1 bay leaf	to garnish
40–45 minutes		1 tsp dried mixed herbs	
		200 g/7 oz live mussels	fresh crusty bread, to serve

Heat the oil and butter in a large pot over a medium heat. Add the garlic and onion and cook, stirring, for 3 minutes. Add the tomatoes, stock, wine, bay leaf and mixed herbs and bring to the boil. Reduce the heat, cover and simmer for 30 minutes. Meanwhile, soak the mussels in a bowl of lightly salted water for 10 minutes. Scrub under cold running water and pull off any beards. Discard any with broken shells. Tap the remaining mussels and discard any that refuse to close. Put the mussels in a large pan with a little water, bring to the boil and cook over a high heat for 4 minutes. Discard any that remain closed.

Rinse the cod under cold water, pat dry with kitchen paper, then cut into chunks. When the tomato mixture has cooked for 30 minutes, add the cod and simmer for 3 minutes. Add the mussels and prawns and cook for 3 minutes. Add the lobster, season, and stir. Simmer for 1 minute. Remove from the heat, discard the bay leaf and ladle into serving bowls. Garnish with parsley and serve with fresh crusty bread.

bouillabaisse

		ingredients	
easy	100 ml/3½ fl oz olive oil	1 tbsp chopped fresh oregano
	3 garlic cloves, chopped	1 tbsp chopped fresh basil
	1 onion, chopped	2 tbsp chopped fresh parsley
serves 4	2 spring onions, trimmed and sliced	200 g/7 oz live mussels
	2 tomatoes, deseeded and chopped	500 g/1 lb 2 oz snapper or
	1 fennel bulb, chopped	monkfish fillets
20 minutes	700 ml/1¼ pints fish stock	200 g/7 oz prawns, peeled and
	400 ml/14 fl oz dry white wine	deveined
	1 bay leaf	salt and pepper
45 minutes	pinch of saffron threads	thick slices of French bread, to serve

Heat the oil in a large pan over a medium heat. Add the garlic, onion and spring onions and cook, stirring, for 3 minutes. Stir in the tomatoes, fennel, stock, wine, bay leaf, saffron and herbs. Bring to the boil, reduce the heat, cover and simmer for 30 minutes.

Meanwhile, soak the mussels in lightly salted water for 10 minutes. Scrub under cold running water and pull off any beards. Discard any with broken shells. Tap the unbroken mussels and discard any that refuse to close. Put the remaining mussels into a large pan with a little water, bring to the boil and cook over a high heat for 4 minutes. Discard any that remain closed.

When the tomato mixture has cooked for 30 minutes, rinse the fish, pat dry with kitchen paper, then cut into small chunks. Add them to the pan and simmer for 5 minutes. Add the mussels and prawns, season, and cook for 3 minutes. Discard the bay leaf and ladle into serving bowls. Serve with thick slices of French bread.

spanish garlic mussels

very easy	
serves 4	
15 minutes	
15–17 minutes	

ingredients

1.8 kg/4 lb live mussels
100 ml/3 ½ fl oz olive oil
6 garlic cloves, finely chopped
250 ml/9 fl oz dry white wine
500 ml/18 fl oz water
juice of 1 lemon
1 tbsp finely grated lemon rind
1 bay leaf

3 tbsp chopped fresh flat-leaved
    parsley
salt and pepper

GARNISH
chopped fresh flat-leaved parsley
wedges of fresh lemon

fresh crusty bread, to serve

Soak the mussels in a bowl of lightly salted water for 10 minutes. Scrub under cold running water and pull off any beards. Discard any with broken shells. Tap the remaining mussels and discard any that refuse to close.

Heat the oil in a large pan over a medium heat. Add the garlic and cook, stirring, for about 3 minutes. Stir in the wine, water, lemon juice and rind and herbs. Season to taste. Bring to the boil, then reduce the heat and simmer for 5 minutes.

Add the mussels, cover and simmer for 5–7 minutes until they have opened. Drain, then discard the bay leaf and any mussels that remain closed. Transfer the mussels to a large serving platter or individual serving plates, scatter over some parsley and lemon wedges, and serve in their shells with some fresh crusty bread.

You can eat these mussels in the traditional Spanish way if you wish, by using one half of a mussel shell as a spoon.

seafood spaghetti

		ingredients	

easy		200 g/7 oz live mussels
		3 tbsp olive oil
		2 garlic cloves, chopped
		6 large tomatoes, deseeded and
		  chopped
			450 g/1 lb dried or fresh spaghetti
			200 g/7 oz cleaned squid, cut into
			  rings and tentacles
			200 g/7 oz canned or freshly cooked
			  crab meat

serves 4		1 tbsp tomato purée 50 g/1¾ oz black olives, stoned and sliced	salt and pepper
15 minutes		100 ml/3½ fl oz red wine 2 tbsp chopped fresh basil	GARNISH sprigs of fresh basil shavings of fresh Parmesan
25 minutes			

Soak the mussels in lightly salted water for 10 minutes. Scrub under cold running water and pull off any beards. Discard any with broken shells and any that refuse to close when tapped. Put the remaining mussels in a large pan with a little water, bring to the boil and cook over a high heat for 4 minutes. Discard any that remain closed.

Heat the oil in a large pan over a medium heat. Add the garlic and cook, stirring, for 3 minutes. Stir in the tomatoes, tomato purée, olives, wine and basil. Bring to the boil, reduce the heat, cover and simmer for 10 minutes. Meanwhile, cook the spaghetti in a large pan of lightly salted boiling water. Cook for 10 minutes if using dried pasta, or 4 minutes if using fresh (check the packet instructions).

Add the mussels, squid and crab to the tomato sauce. Season, then cook for 3 minutes. Drain the pasta and transfer to individual serving plates. Pour the seafood sauce over the pasta. Garnish with sprigs of fresh basil and Parmesan shavings.

chicken with herbs & garlic

		ingredients	
easy	2 tbsp olive oil	100 ml/3½ fl oz chicken stock
	2 tbsp butter	2 tbsp lemon juice
serves 4	2 garlic cloves, chopped	4 potatoes, sliced
	1 large onion, chopped	4 carrots, sliced
	2 shallots, chopped	1 bay leaf
	4 skinless, boneless chicken breasts,	salt and pepper
15 minutes	cut into bite-sized pieces	
	1 tsp ground coriander	chopped fresh coriander and parsley,
	2 tbsp chopped fresh coriander	to garnish
50 minutes	100 ml/3½ fl oz dry white wine	fresh crusty bread, to serve

Heat the oil and butter in a large saucepan over a medium heat. Add the garlic, onion and shallots and cook, stirring, for about 3 minutes, until slightly softened.

Add the chicken and ground and fresh coriander and cook, stirring frequently, for 10 minutes. Lower the heat, cover the pan and cook gently for 10 minutes.

Pour in the wine, chicken stock and lemon juice, then add the potatoes, carrots and bay leaf. Season with salt and pepper and bring to the boil. Reduce the heat, cover and simmer for about 25 minutes, stirring occasionally.

Remove from the heat, discard the bay leaf and transfer to serving dishes. Garnish with chopped fresh coriander and parsley and serve with fresh crusty bread.

baked chicken in red wine

		ingredients	
	very easy	3 tbsp olive oil	2 tbsp chopped fresh basil
		2 garlic cloves, chopped	1 tsp dried mixed herbs
	serves 4	4 tomatoes, deseeded and chopped	salt and pepper
		1 tbsp tomato purée	4 skinless, boneless chicken breasts
		2 tbsp sherry vinegar	
	10 minutes	6 tbsp red wine	sprigs of fresh basil, to garnish
		12 black olives, stoned and halved	fresh crusty bread, to serve
		1 tbsp capers	
	1 hour		

Preheat the oven to 180°C/350°F/Gas Mark 4. Heat the oil in a pan over a low heat. Add the garlic and cook, stirring, for 4 minutes or until slightly softened.

Add the tomatoes, tomato purée, vinegar, wine, olives, capers and herbs. Season with salt and pepper. Bring to the boil, then reduce the heat, cover the pan, and simmer for about 10 minutes.

Arrange the chicken in the bottom of an ovenproof baking dish. Remove the tomato sauce from the heat and pour it over the chicken. Bake in the preheated oven for 45 minutes, basting the chicken with sauce from time to time.

Remove from the oven. Divide the chicken between individual serving plates, pour tomato sauce over the top, then garnish with fresh basil sprigs and serve with fresh crusty bread.

chicken provençal with linguine

		ingredients	
easy		1 aubergine, about 250 g/9 oz	12 black olives, stoned and quartered
		3 tbsp olive oil	100 g/3½ oz canned anchovy fillets in
serves 4		4 skinless, boneless chicken breasts,	oil, drained and sliced
		cut into bite-sized pieces	1 tsp dried mixed herbs
		2 garlic cloves, chopped	450 g/1 lb dried or fresh linguine
		1 large onion, chopped	salt and pepper
35 minutes		250 g/9 oz white mushrooms, sliced	
		4 large tomatoes, skinned (see page 8)	fresh basil leaves, to garnish
		and chopped	
35–40 minutes		100 ml/3½ fl oz dry white wine	

Trim and slice the aubergine, then put it into a colander. Sprinkle with salt and set aside for 30 minutes.

Heat 2 tablespoons of oil in a large pan over a medium heat. Add the chicken pieces and cook, stirring, for 4 minutes. Using a slotted spoon, lift out the chicken and set aside. Heat the remaining oil in the pan, add the chopped garlic and onion and cook, stirring, for 3 minutes. Add the mushrooms and chicken. Rinse the aubergine, pat dry with kitchen paper and add to the pan with the tomatoes, wine and olives. Cook, stirring, for 15 minutes. Add the anchovies and mixed herbs. Cook, stirring, for 10 minutes.

Meanwhile, cook the linguine in a pan of lightly salted boiling water. Cook for 10 minutes if using dried pasta, or 4 minutes if using fresh (check the packet instructions), until tender but firm to the bite. Drain and divide between serving plates. Spoon the chicken and sauce over the pasta. Garnish with basil leaves and serve.

moroccan spiced chicken

		ingredients	
easy	1 aubergine, about 250 g/9 oz, trimmed and thickly sliced	1 tsp powdered ginger
		1 tsp powdered saffron
serves 4	700 ml/1 ¼ pints chicken stock	½ tsp nutmeg
	4 skinless, boneless chicken breasts	3 large carrots, chopped
	4 tbsp butter	salt and pepper
35 minutes	4 tbsp olive oil	4 courgettes, trimmed and chopped
	1 onion, sliced	450 g/1 lb canned chickpeas
	1 kg/2 lb 4 oz tomatoes	400 ml/14 fl oz water
50 minutes	1 small red chilli, deseeded and chopped	350 g/12 oz couscous
	4 tbsp chopped fresh coriander	sprigs of fresh parsley, to garnish

Sprinkle the aubergine with salt. Set aside for 30 minutes. Bring the stock to the boil in a large pan. Add the chicken and cook over a low heat for 20 minutes. Lift it out and set aside. Reserve the stock. Melt half the butter with all the oil in a large pot. Add the onion and cook over a medium heat, stirring, for 3 minutes. Add the tomatoes, chilli, coriander, spices and seasoning. Cook for 1 minute. Rinse the aubergine, pat dry, cut into bite-sized pieces and add to the pot with the carrots, courgettes, stock, and the canned chickpeas with their liquid. Bring to the boil, cover and simmer for 20 minutes.

Meanwhile, put the water and remaining butter into a large pan and bring to the boil. Stir in the couscous, remove from the heat and soak for 10 minutes. Two minutes before the end of soaking, add the chicken to the sauce and cook for 2 minutes. Pile the couscous onto individual serving plates. Lift out the chicken and arrange on the couscous, pour over the sauce and garnish with sprigs of fresh parsley.

lamb kebabs

		ingredients	
very easy		625 g/1 lb 6 oz minced lamb	16 cherry tomatoes
		90 g/3¼ oz Gruyère cheese, grated	1 tbsp olive oil
serves 4		4 tbsp thick natural yogurt	
		2 garlic cloves, chopped	sprigs of fresh rosemary, to garnish
		1 tbsp chopped fresh rosemary	freshly cooked rice, to serve
15 minutes		salt and pepper	
		16 button mushrooms	
10 minutes			

In a large bowl, mix together the lamb, cheese, yogurt and garlic. Stir in the rosemary and season with salt and pepper. Using your hands, shape the mixture into small balls.

Thread the lamb balls onto skewers, alternating them with the mushrooms and cherry tomatoes. When the skewers are full (leave a small space at either end), brush them with oil. Transfer them to a preheated grill or a barbecue. Cook for about 10 minutes or until cooked right through, turning them frequently and brushing with more oil when necessary.

Remove from the heat and serve with freshly cooked rice, garnished with sprigs of rosemary.

provençal stew

		ingredients	
easy		3 tbsp olive oil	6 green olives, stoned and quartered
		750 g/1 lb 10 oz lean stewing steak, cubed	salt and pepper
serves 4		2 garlic cloves, chopped	400 ml/14 fl oz red wine
		1 large onion, chopped	200 ml/7 fl oz vegetable stock
15 minutes		250 g/9 oz white mushrooms, sliced	sprig of fresh flat-leaved parsley, to garnish
		4 large tomatoes, skinned (see page 8) and chopped	
2 hours		2 carrots, sliced	fresh crusty bread, to serve
		6 black olives, stoned and quartered	

Preheat the oven to 160°C/325°F/Gas Mark 3. Heat 2 tablespoons of the oil in a flameproof casserole. Add the meat and cook, stirring, over a high heat for about 5 minutes or until sealed. Remove from the heat. Using a slotted spoon, lift out the meat and set aside.

Heat the remaining oil in the casserole. Add the garlic and onion and cook, stirring, over a medium heat for about 4 minutes until softened slightly. Add the mushrooms and tomatoes and cook for a further 5 minutes, stirring frequently.

Return the meat to the casserole, then add the carrots and olives and season to taste with salt and pepper. Pour in the wine and stock, bring to the boil, then reduce the heat and simmer for 15 minutes. Transfer to the preheated oven and cook for 1½ hours. Garnish with a sprig of parsley and serve with fresh crusty bread.

vegetarian
& salads

Vegetarian cuisine is absolutely in its element in the Mediterranean, with the wonderful fruits and vegetables, cheeses, nuts, oils and herbs available in the region, so what better way to show off than with a dazzling extravaganza of Mediterranean vegetarian dishes? This chapter is bursting with luscious temptations, from irresistible pizzas, polenta, pasta and salads to the legendary Imam Bayildi from Turkey – a dish reputed to be so delicious that it made a holy man swoon with delight.

ratatouille

		ingredients	
very easy		1 aubergine, about 250 g/9 oz	1 tsp sugar
		4 tbsp olive oil	2 tbsp chopped fresh thyme
serves 4		2 garlic cloves, chopped	salt and pepper
		1 large onion, chopped	
		2 red peppers, deseeded and cut into	sprigs of fresh thyme, to garnish
		bite-sized chunks	TO SERVE
35 minutes		800 g/1 lb 12 oz canned chopped	freshly baked jacket potatoes
		tomatoes	with butter
		2 courgettes, trimmed and sliced	fresh crusty bread
45 minutes		1 celery stick, trimmed and sliced	

Trim the aubergine and cut it into bite-sized chunks, then put it into a colander. Sprinkle the aubergine with salt and set aside for about 30 minutes.

Heat the oil in a large saucepan over a medium heat. Add the garlic and onion and cook, stirring, for about 3 minutes until softened slightly. Rinse the aubergine and drain well, then add it to the pan with the red peppers. Reduce the heat and cook gently, stirring frequently, for another 10 minutes.

Stir in the tomatoes, courgettes, celery, sugar and thyme, and season with salt and pepper. Bring to the boil, then lower the heat, cover the pan, and simmer gently for about 30 minutes.

Remove from the heat, transfer to serving plates and garnish with sprigs of fresh thyme. Serve with buttered hot jacket potatoes and fresh crusty bread.

felafel with tahini

		ingredients	
easy	450 g/1 lb canned haricot beans	TAHINI SAUCE
	350 g/12 oz canned chickpeas	200 ml/7 fl oz tahini
serves 4	1 onion, finely chopped	1 garlic clove, chopped
	2 garlic cloves, chopped	1–2 tbsp water
	1 small red chilli, deseeded and chopped	2–3 tsp lemon juice
15 minutes	1 tsp baking powder	
	25 g/1 oz chopped fresh parsley	sprigs of fresh parsley, to garnish
	pinch of cayenne	TO SERVE
10 minutes	2 tbsp water	pitta bread
	salt and pepper	thick natural yogurt or tzatziki
	vegetable oil, for deep-frying	(see page 18)

To make the tahini sauce, put the tahini into a bowl then add the garlic. Gradually stir in the water until a fairly smooth consistency is reached, then stir in lemon juice to taste. Add more water or lemon juice if necessary. Cover with clingfilm and chill.

To make the felafel, rinse and drain the haricot beans and chickpeas. Put them into a food processor with the onion, garlic, chilli, baking powder, parsley and cayenne. Process to a rough paste, then add the water and season with plenty of salt and pepper. Process again briefly.

Heat about 6 cm/2 ½ inches of oil in a deep-fryer or a large, heavy-bottomed saucepan. Fry rounded tablespoonfuls of the mixture in the hot oil for about 2–2 ½ minutes until golden and crispy on the outside (you will need to do this in batches). Drain well on kitchen paper and garnish with sprigs of fresh parsley. Serve hot or cold with tahini sauce, pitta bread, and yogurt or tzatziki.

imam bayildi

easy	
serves 4	
35 minutes + 20 minutes to cool	
1¼ hours	

ingredients

2 aubergines, about 275 g/9½ oz each
6 tbsp olive oil
3 garlic cloves, chopped
2 onions, chopped
750 g/1 lb 10 oz canned chopped
   tomatoes
2 red peppers, deseeded and chopped
1 celery stick, trimmed and sliced
1 tbsp raisins
1 tbsp sultanas

pinch of nutmeg
1 tbsp chopped fresh flat-leaved
   parsley
salt and pepper

sprigs of fresh flat-leaved parsley,
   to garnish

freshly cooked rice, to serve

Cut each aubergine lengthways. Scoop out the flesh, leaving 1 cm/ ½ inch of flesh round the inside of each half. Chop the flesh. Sprinkle the flesh and halves with salt. Leave for 30 minutes.

Heat 3 tablespoons of oil in a pan over a medium heat. Add the garlic and onion and cook, stirring, for 3 minutes. Rinse the aubergine flesh and drain it; add to the pan, with the tomatoes. Cook, stirring, for 10 minutes. Preheat the oven to 180°C/350°F/Gas Mark 4. Add the red peppers, celery, raisins, sultanas, nutmeg and parsley to the pan. Season, lower the heat, cover and simmer for 15 minutes.

Place the aubergine halves in an ovenproof dish. Spoon the tomato mixture into the halves. Drizzle with oil, cover with foil, and bake for 45 minutes. Remove from the oven and leave to cool to room temperature. Garnish with parsley and serve with freshly cooked rice. Alternatively, to serve cold, let the aubergines cool completely, cover with clingfilm and chill. Bring them out 1 hour before serving.

vegetable polenta

very easy		
serves 4		
35 minutes		
1 hour		

ingredients

1 aubergine, about 250 g/9 oz, trimmed and sliced
300 g/10½ oz polenta
1.2 litres/2 pints vegetable stock
6 tbsp olive oil
1 garlic clove, chopped
2 red onions, sliced
850 g/1 lb 14 oz small new potatoes, halved

1 red pepper, cut into strips
1 orange pepper, cut into strips
2 courgettes, deseeded and sliced
3 tbsp sun-dried tomatoes in oil, drained and chopped
1 tbsp chopped fresh rosemary
1 tbsp chopped fresh parsley
salt and pepper

sprigs of fresh flat-leaved parsley, to garnish

Sprinkle the aubergine slices with salt and set aside for 30 minutes.

Preheat the oven to 190°C/375°F/Gas Mark 5, then oil an ovenproof dish. Put the polenta and stock into a large pan and bring to the boil, stirring constantly. Boil for 10 minutes, stirring, then transfer to the oiled dish. Bake for 45 minutes, turning the polenta over halfway through. Meanwhile, heat 3 tablespoons of the oil in a large pan over a medium heat. Add the garlic and onion and cook, stirring, for 3 minutes. Rinse the aubergine, pat dry and add to the pan with the potatoes, peppers, courgettes, tomatoes, rosemary and parsley. Season. Cook for 5 minutes, then lower the heat and cook, stirring, for 10 minutes.

Lightly oil a baking sheet and spread out the vegetables on it. Drizzle over the remaining oil, then roast in the oven for 20 minutes, turning them over halfway through the cooking time. Remove the polenta from the oven, cut it into wedges and arrange with the roasted vegetables on serving plates. Garnish with sprigs of parsley and serve.

tomato & mozzarella pizzas

		ingredients	
easy		2 red onions	1 tsp butter
		3 tbsp olive oil	200 g/7 oz white mushrooms, sliced
serves 4		2 garlic cloves, chopped	1 tbsp plain flour, to dust
		400 g/14 oz canned chopped tomatoes	2 ready-prepared pizza bases, about
		1 tbsp chopped fresh oregano	23 cm/9 inches in diameter
		1 tsp dried mixed herbs	300 g/10½ oz mozzarella, chopped
10 minutes		1 bay leaf	4 tomatoes, sliced
		2½ tbsp tomato purée	1 red pepper, cut into thin strips
40–45 minutes		½ tsp sugar	fresh basil leaves, to garnish
		salt and pepper	

Chop one onion, slice the other, and set aside. Heat 1½ tablespoons of oil in a large pan. Add one of the garlic cloves and the chopped onion (reserve the sliced onion) and cook, stirring, over a medium heat for 3 minutes. Add the canned tomatoes and the herbs, tomato purée and sugar. Season and bring to the boil, stirring. Lower the heat and simmer, uncovered, for 15 minutes.

Preheat the oven to 190°C/375°F/Gas Mark 5. Melt the butter in a pan over a medium heat. Add the mushrooms and cook, stirring, for 5 minutes, then drain. Remove the sauce from the heat and discard the bay leaf.

Lightly flour two baking sheets and place a pizza base on each one. Spread tomato sauce over each base. Scatter over the mozzarella, remaining garlic and sliced onion. Arrange the mushrooms, tomatoes and pepper over the top, and drizzle over the remaining oil. Bake for 20–25 minutes. Remove from the oven and garnish with basil leaves.

creamy mushroom tagliatelle

		ingredients	
	very easy	50 g/1¾ oz pine kernels	2 tbsp chopped fresh basil
		400 g/14 oz dried or fresh tagliatelle	250 g/9 oz mascarpone cheese
	serves 4	75 g/2¾ oz frozen peas	salt and pepper
		2 tbsp butter	
		400 g/14 oz white mushrooms, sliced	GARNISH
	10 minutes		4 tbsp freshly grated Parmesan
			fresh basil leaves
	15 minutes		

Bring two pans of lightly salted water to the boil. Meanwhile, cook the pine kernels in a dry frying pan over a low heat, stirring, for 1–2 minutes until golden. Transfer to a small plate and set aside.

Put the pasta in one pan of boiling water and put the peas in the other. Cook the pasta over a low heat for about 10 minutes if using dried, or about 4 minutes if using fresh (check the packet instructions), until tender but still firm to the bite. Cook the peas over a low heat for 5 minutes.

While the pasta and peas are cooking, melt the butter in a frying pan, add the mushrooms and cook, stirring, for 4–5 minutes until tender. Remove from the heat and drain any excess liquid. Drain the pasta and peas and transfer them to a large bowl. Add the pine kernels, mushrooms and basil. Stir in the mascarpone, season with salt and pepper, then divide between individual serving plates. Scatter over the grated Parmesan and fresh basil leaves and serve.

vegetable moussaka

		ingredients	
very easy		2 aubergines, about 250 g/9 oz each, peeled and cut into chunks	salt and pepper
			300 g/10½ oz potatoes, sliced
serves 4		5 tbsp olive oil, plus extra for greasing	125 ml/4 fl oz single cream
		2 garlic cloves, chopped	175 g/6 oz ricotta cheese
		1 large onion, chopped	2 eggs, beaten
		1 red pepper, deseeded and chopped	
35 minutes		1 green pepper, deseeded and chopped	GARNISH
		400 g/14 oz canned chopped tomatoes	pinch of cayenne
		1 courgette, trimmed and sliced	sprigs of fresh rosemary
1 hour		1 tbsp chopped fresh rosemary	fresh crusty bread, to serve

Sprinkle the aubergine chunks with salt and set aside for 30 minutes.

Heat the oil in a large pan over a medium heat. Add the garlic and onion and cook, stirring, for 3 minutes. Add the red and green peppers and cook for 5 minutes. Rinse the aubergine, drain, then add to the pan. Reduce the heat and cook, stirring, for 10 minutes.

Preheat the oven to 200°C/400°F/Gas Mark 6. Stir the tomatoes, courgette and rosemary into the aubergines. Season, bring to the boil, then lower the heat, cover, and simmer gently for 10 minutes. Meanwhile, bring a pan of lightly salted water to the boil, add the sliced potatoes and cook over a medium heat for 5 minutes. Drain.

Mix the cream, ricotta and eggs in a bowl. Oil an ovenproof dish and spoon in the aubergine mixture. Top with the potatoes. Pour over the ricotta sauce. Bake for 30 minutes. Remove from the oven and divide between individual serving plates. Garnish with cayenne and sprigs of rosemary. Serve with crusty bread.

moroccan spiced salad

		ingredients	
	very easy	2 tbsp olive oil	½ tsp mustard
		90 g/3 ¼ oz long-grain rice	225 g/8 oz canned red kidney beans
	serves 4	400 ml/14 fl oz water	225 g/8 oz canned chickpeas
		4 tbsp lemon-flavoured or extra-virgin olive oil	2 shallots, chopped
			4 spring onions, trimmed and sliced
	15 minutes	3 tbsp vinegar	60 g/2 ¼ oz pine kernels
		1 tbsp lemon juice	100 g/3 ½ oz sultanas
		1 tbsp honey	1 tbsp chopped fresh mint
	40 minutes	1 tsp garam masala	chopped fresh mint, to garnish
		1 tsp ground coriander	wedges of fresh lemon, to serve

Heat the olive oil in a large saucepan. Add the rice and cook for 3 minutes, stirring, over a low heat. Pour in the water and bring to the boil, then lower the heat, cover and simmer for 35 minutes. Remove from the heat and transfer to a colander. Rinse under cold running water, drain well and set aside to cool.

In a large bowl, mix together the lemon-flavoured oil or extra-virgin olive oil, vinegar, lemon juice and honey. Add the garam masala, coriander and mustard and stir well.

Add the rice and mix well. Rinse and drain the kidney beans and chickpeas, then add them to the bowl with the shallots, spring onions, pine kernels, sultanas and mint. Divide the salad between serving bowls, garnish with chopped fresh mint and serve with lemon wedges.

avocado salad

		ingredients	
extremely easy			

serves 4	large handful of radicchio leaves
	large handful of rocket leaves
	1 small galia melon
	2 ripe avocados
	1 tbsp lemon juice
	200 g/7 oz fontina cheese, cut into
	  bite-sized pieces
		DRESSING
		5 tbsp lemon-flavoured or extra-virgin
		  olive oil
		1 tbsp white wine vinegar
		1 tbsp lemon juice
		1 tbsp chopped fresh parsley	

15 minutes			
—			

To make the dressing, mix together the oil, vinegar, lemon juice and parsley in a small bowl.

Arrange the radicchio and rocket on serving plates. Halve and deseed the melon, then cut the flesh from the skin. Discard the skin. Slice the melon flesh and arrange it over the salad leaves.

Cut the avocados in half and remove and discard the stones and skin. Slice the flesh and brush with lemon juice. Arrange the slices over the melon, then scatter over the cheese. Drizzle over the dressing, garnish with chopped fresh parsley and serve.

greek salad

		ingredients	
extremely easy		4 tomatoes, cut into wedges	½ tsp sugar
		1 onion, sliced	1 tbsp chopped fresh coriander
serves 4		½ cucumber, sliced	salt and pepper
		225 g/8 oz kalamata olives, stoned	
		225 g/8 oz feta cheese, cubed	fresh flat-leaved parsley, to garnish
15 minutes		2 tbsp fresh coriander leaves	pitta bread, to serve
		DRESSING	
		5 tbsp extra-virgin olive oil	
—		2 tbsp white wine vinegar	
		1 tbsp lemon juice	

To make the dressing, put the oil, vinegar, lemon juice, sugar and coriander into a large bowl. Season with salt and pepper and mix together well.

Add the tomatoes, onion, cucumber, olives, cheese and coriander. Toss all the ingredients together, then divide between individual serving bowls. Garnish with fresh parsley and serve with pitta bread.

italian salad

		ingredients	
	extremely easy	225 g/8 oz dried conchiglie (pasta shells)	DRESSING
		50 g/1¾ oz pine kernels	5 tbsp extra-virgin olive oil
	serves 4	350 g/12 oz cherry tomatoes, halved	2 tbsp balsamic vinegar
		1 red pepper, deseeded and cut into bite-sized chunks	1 tbsp chopped fresh basil
	15 minutes	1 red onion, chopped	salt and pepper
		200 g/7 oz buffalo mozzarella, cut into small pieces	shavings of fresh Parmesan, to garnish
	10–15 minutes	12 black olives, stoned	
		25 g/1 oz fresh basil leaves	

Bring a large saucepan of lightly salted water to the boil. Add the pasta and cook over a medium heat for about 10 minutes, or according to the packet instructions. When cooked, the pasta should be tender but still firm to the bite. Drain, rinse under cold running water and drain again. Leave to cool.

While the pasta is cooking, put the pine kernels in a dry frying pan and cook over a low heat for 1–2 minutes until golden brown. Remove from the heat, transfer to a dish and leave to cool.

To make the dressing, put the oil, vinegar and basil into a small bowl. Season with salt and pepper and stir together well. Cover with clingfilm and set to one side.

To assemble the salad, divide the pasta between serving bowls. Add the pine kernels, tomatoes, red pepper, onion, cheese and olives. Scatter over the basil leaves, then drizzle over the dressing. Garnish with fresh Parmesan shavings and serve.

desserts

This chapter offers a truly wonderful
array of desserts, from cool, refreshing
concoctions such as Orange Sorbet to
deliciously satisfying cakes from Italy. For
the sweet-toothed there's a superb Baklava,
the famed dessert of Greece and Turkey,
and if chocolate is your passion you need
look no further than the Tiramisù, which
combines the tantalising flavours of coffee,
chocolate, orange and cream. So whatever
your taste, and however you wish to finish
your meal, there is bound to be a dessert
here to suit the occasion.

orange sorbet

		ingredients
easy		500 ml/18 fl oz water
		200 g/7 oz caster sugar
serves 4		4 large oranges
		2 tbsp orange liqueur, such as Cointreau
1¾–4 hours		4 scooped-out oranges, to serve
4 minutes		

Heat the water and sugar in a pan over a low heat, stirring, until dissolved. Boil without stirring for 2 minutes. Pour into a heatproof bowl. Cool to room temperature. Grate the rind from 2 oranges and extract the juice. Extract the juice from 2 more oranges. Mix the juice and rind in a bowl, cover with clingfilm, and set aside. Discard the squeezed oranges. Stir the orange juice, grated rind and orange liqueur into the cooled syrup. Cover with clingfilm and chill for 1 hour. Transfer to an ice-cream maker and process for 15 minutes.

If you do not have an ice-cream maker, use the following freezer method. Put the mixture in a freezerproof container. Freeze for 1 hour, then transfer to a bowl. Beat to break up the crystals, then put it back in the freezerproof container and freeze for 30 minutes. Repeat twice more, freezing for 30 minutes and whisking each time.

Divide the frozen sorbet between the scooped-out orange cups and serve at once.

chocolate gelato

		ingredients
easy		6 egg yolks
		100 g/3½ oz caster sugar
serves 4		350ml/12 fl oz milk
		175 ml/6 fl oz double cream
		90 g/3¼ oz cooking chocolate, grated
1¾–4 hours		pieces of flaked chocolate, or caraque
		(see below), to decorate
4 minutes		

Beat the egg yolks and sugar in a large, heatproof bowl until fluffy. Pour the milk, cream and grated chocolate into a large pan and bring to the boil. Remove from the heat and whisk into the beaten egg yolks. Pour back into the pan and cook, stirring, over a very low heat until thickened. Do not let it reach a simmer. Transfer to a bowl and cool. Cover with clingfilm and chill for 1 hour.

Transfer to an ice-cream maker and process for 15 minutes. If you do not have an ice-cream maker, use the freezer method (see page 84).

If you are using caraque for decoration, you can make your own as follows. Melt some chocolate in a heatproof bowl placed over a pan of simmering water, then spread it over an acrylic board and leave to set. Scrape a knife over the chocolate to form the caraque.

To serve, scoop the gelato into serving dishes. Decorate with pieces of flaked chocolate, or caraque if using.

baklava

<table>
<tr><td>very easy</td><td colspan="2" align="center">ingredients</td></tr>
<tr><td rowspan="2">serves 4</td><td>150 g/5½ oz shelled pistachio nuts, finely chopped</td><td>150 g/5½ oz butter, melted, plus extra for greasing</td></tr>
<tr><td>75 g/2¾ oz toasted hazelnuts, finely chopped</td><td>250 g/9 oz (about 16 sheets) frozen filo pastry, defrosted</td></tr>
<tr><td rowspan="2">20 minutes</td><td>75 g/2¾ oz blanched hazelnuts, finely chopped</td><td>250 ml/9 fl oz water</td></tr>
<tr><td>grated rind of 1 lemon</td><td>2 tbsp honey</td></tr>
<tr><td rowspan="2">1 hour</td><td>1 tbsp brown sugar</td><td>1 tbsp lemon juice</td></tr>
<tr><td>1 tsp mixed spice</td><td>300 g/10½ oz caster sugar
½ tsp cinnamon</td></tr>
</table>

Preheat the oven to 160°C/325°F/Gas Mark 3. Put the nuts, lemon rind, sugar and mixed spice into a bowl and mix well. Grease a round cake tin, 18 cm/7 inches in diameter and 5 cm/2 inches deep, with butter. Cut the whole stack of filo sheets to the size of the tin. Keep the filo circles covered with a damp tea towel. Lay 1 circle on the bottom of the tin and brush with melted butter. Add another 6 circles on top, brushing between each layer with melted butter. Spread over one-third of the nut mixture, then add 3 circles of buttered filo. Spread over another third of nut mixture then top with 3 more circles of buttered filo. Spread over the remaining nut mixture and add the last 3 circles of buttered filo. Cut into wedges, then bake for 1 hour.

Meanwhile, put the water, honey, lemon juice, caster sugar and cinnamon into a pan. Bring to the boil, stirring. Lower the heat and simmer, without stirring, for 15 minutes. Cool. Remove the baklava from the oven, pour over the syrup and leave to set before serving.

tiramisù

		ingredients	
	very easy	200 ml/7 fl oz strong black coffee, cooled to room temperature	3 tbsp icing sugar
			grated rind of 1 orange
	serves 4	4 tbsp orange liqueur, such as Cointreau	60 g/2¼ oz chocolate, grated
		3 tbsp orange juice	DECORATION
	20 minutes + 2 hours to chill	16 Italian sponge fingers	chopped toasted almonds
		250 g/9 oz mascarpone cheese	crystallised orange peel
		300 ml/10 fl oz double cream, lightly whipped	
	—		

Pour the cooled coffee into a jug and stir in the orange liqueur and orange juice. Put 8 of the sponge fingers in the bottom of a serving dish, then pour over half of the coffee mixture.

Put the mascarpone in a separate bowl along with the cream, icing sugar and orange rind and mix together well. Spread half of the mascarpone mixture over the coffee-soaked sponge fingers, then arrange the remaining sponge fingers on top. Pour over the remaining coffee mixture and then spread over the remaining mascarpone mixture. Scatter over the grated chocolate and chill in the refrigerator for at least 2 hours. Serve decorated with chopped toasted almonds and crystallised orange peel.

sicilian citrus cake

		ingredients	
very easy		1 tsp olive oil, for greasing	TOPPING
		225 g/8 oz plain flour	250 ml/9 fl oz double cream, whipped
serves 4		1 tsp baking powder	3 tbsp icing sugar
		1 tsp bicarbonate of soda	1 tbsp grated orange rind
		pinch of salt	
20 minutes		150 g/5½ oz caster sugar	strips of crystallised orange and
		2 eggs	lemon peel, to decorate
		finely grated rind and juice of 1 orange	
45 minutes		2 tbsp limoncello (lemon liqueur) or	
		orange liqueur such as Cointreau	

Preheat the oven to 180°C/350°F/Gas Mark 4. Grease a round 20-cm/8-inch cake tin with oil and line it with baking paper.

Sift the flour, baking powder, bicarbonate of soda and salt into a large mixing bowl, then stir in the caster sugar.

In a separate bowl, mix the eggs with the orange rind and juice. Stir in the limoncello or orange liqueur, then pour the mixture into the flour and stir well.

Transfer the mixture to the prepared cake tin, smooth the surface and bake in the centre of the preheated oven for at least 45 minutes, until firm and golden. Remove from the oven and leave to cool, then turn out the cake onto a serving plate.

To make the topping, put the cream into a bowl and add the icing sugar and orange rind. Mix well, then spread over the top of the cake. Decorate with crystallised orange and lemon peel and serve.

golden polenta cake

		ingredients	
	very easy	100 g/3½ oz butter, plus extra for greasing	50 g/1¾ oz chopped almonds
		90 g/3¼ oz caster sugar	grated rind and juice of 1 orange
	serves 4	2 eggs, beaten	
		50 g/1¾ oz self-raising flour	DECORATION
		1 tsp baking powder	icing sugar
	20 minutes	100 g/3½ oz polenta	toasted flaked almonds
		150 g/5½ oz sultanas	mascarpone cheese, to serve
	45 minutes		

Preheat the oven to 180°C/350°F/Gas Mark 4. Grease a round 20-cm/8-inch cake tin and line it with baking paper.

Cream together the butter and caster sugar in a bowl, then gradually whisk in the beaten eggs. Fold in the flour, baking powder and polenta. Add the sultanas, almonds and the orange rind and juice, and stir together well.

Transfer the mixture to the prepared cake tin and smooth the surface. Bake in the centre of the preheated oven for 45 minutes until firm and golden. Remove from the oven and leave to cool, then turn out the cake onto a serving plate.

Sprinkle over the icing sugar and flaked almonds and serve with generous spoonfuls of mascarpone.

index